CATHOLIC GREAT BOOKS STUDY GUIDES

G. K. CHESTERTON

LEPANTO

An Integrated Literature/History Course

By Julie A. Collorafi

LITTLE LATIN

READERS

www.littlelatinreaders.com

Front cover illustration: "Allegory of the Battle of Lepanto," by Paul Veronese, 1571. Original in the Doge's Palace, Venice. Heaven takes part in the great naval battle; Our Lord and Our Lady spread light on the Christian forces and darkness on the Turks. Sts. Peter, Mark, Roch and Justine intercede on behalf of the Catholic European nations.

NOTES TO THE TEACHER

This enrichment course on Chesterton's *Lepanto* is designed to supplement an already-existing European or Church history course. It could also be used in a poetry or English literature course. The study guide includes a suggested lesson plan, an optional test, and an answer key which provides the answers for the questions in the guide and for the test, and for the discussion questions on the optional supplement, *St. Pius V,* a short biography of Pope Pius V written by Robin Anderson, available from Tan Books.

A Lesson Plan provided on the next two pages gives all the daily assignments. The optional test on p. 28-32 is is recommended as a way to help the student formulate his own conclusions about the poem. The Answer Key, starting on p. 33, is provided as a tool to aid the student's understanding and should be consulted as necessary, especially if the student is having difficulty understanding the section on poetic devices and meter.

After the work in the study guide has been completed, the student can prepare for the test by going over the review questions provided on p. 24 of the guide. If the student is going on to read *St. Pius V*, there are a few discussion questions for each chapter, on p. 24-25. The answers to these are also in the answer key.

I hope your student will enjoy this journey back to one of the most exciting moments in the Church's history, a moment when the fate of Christendom seemed to hang in the balance and the faith of the brave few who responded was rewarded in a truly miraculous manner.

SUGGESTED LESSON PLAN

WEEK 1, DAY 1
Read the Introduction p. 1-3 in the study guide. Read "The Background" on p. 51-57 of the text. Answer the five questions on p. 3-4 of the study guide.

WEEK 1, DAY 2
Read "The Battle" on p. 39-69 in the text and answer the questions in the study guide on p. 4-5.

WEEK 1, DAY 3
Read "The Aftermath" on p. 71-75 in text and answer the questions on p. 6 in the study guide.

WEEK 1, DAY 4
Read "The Poem" in the text on p. 77-88 and answer the five questions on p. 7 in the study guide.

WEEK 2, DAY 1
Read *Lepanto* on the gray-edged pages in the text.

WEEK 2, DAY 2
Read "Structure and Poetic Elements" on p. 7-12 in the study guide. Complete the Practice sections on p. 9-10 and p. 12.

WEEK 2, DAY 3
Read endnotes for Stanza 1 on p. 18-22 in the text and then read the first stanza again. Answer questions in the guide on p.13-14.

WEEK 2, DAY 4
Read endnotes for Stanza 2 on p. 22-24 in text and read the second stanza. Answer the questions on p. 14-15 in the guide.

WEEK 3, DAY 1
Read the notes for Stanza 3 on p. 24-27 in text and read the third stanza. Answer the questions in the guide on p. 15-16.

WEEK 3, DAY 2
Read the notes for Stanza 4 on p. 27-32 in the text and read the fourth stanza. Answer the questions on p. 16-17 in the guide.

WEEK 3, DAY 3
Read the notes for Stanza 5 on p. 32-35 in the text and read the fifth stanza. Answer the questions in the guide on p. 17-18.

WEEK 3, DAY 4
Read the notes for Stanza 6 on p. 35-38 in the text and read the sixth stanza. Answer the questions in the guide on p. 19.

WEEK 4, DAY 1
Read the notes for Stanza 7 in the text on p.39-44 and read the seventh stanza. Answer the questions in the guide on p. 20-21.

WEEK 4, DAY 2
Read the notes in the text for Stanza 8 on p. 44-47 and read the eighth and final stanza. Answer the questions on p.21-22 in the guide. This completes the work on *Lepanto*.

WEEK 4, DAY 3
Prepare for the test by going over the Review Questions in the guide on p. 24.

WEEK 4, DAY 4
Take the test on p. 29-33.

WEEK 5, DAY 1 (OPTIONAL)
Read the first two chapters in *St. Pius V,* p. 1-26, and answer the discussion questions on p. 25.

WEEK 5, DAY 2
Read Chapters 3 and 4 in *St. Pius V* on p. 27-53 and answer questions on p. 25 in the guide.

WEEK 5, DAY 3
Read Chapters 5 and 6 in *St. Pius V* on p. 54-83 and answer questions on p. 26 in the guide.

WEEK 5, DAY 4
Read the last two chapters in *St. Pius V* on p. 84-100 and answer the questions on p. 26 in the guide.

LEPANTO

I n the spiral of events after the terrorist attack on the World Trade Center, much attention has been focused on the threat of Islam to western Europe and the United States. Any student of history is quick to realize that this threat is not a new one, and that in the Middle Ages the threat was much greater and more perilous than what we face now. The danger then was not random acts of terror, as terrifying as that could be, but rather the entire *conquest* of Europe itself.

What Western civilization would be like now if Islam had succeeded then is not difficult to imagine. Observe any Muslim nation to see what it would be like, principally, the oppression of women and the suppression and persecution of Christians.

From the 1200's to the 1300's, four Crusades were fought by Christian knights from Europe in the Holy Land, attempting to protect the city of Jerusalem and other places sacred to Christians from being taking over by the Moors.

The Crusades were a failure on many counts, but they did manage to preserve Jerusalem and, most importantly, they halted the spread of Islam for a time. However, by the 1500's, Islam was on the rise again, this time threatening to engulf Europe itself via Italy and the eastern European borders. Serious inroads had been made in Spain, and it took most of Spain's effort to stem the tide there.

What was so vital at this moment in history was the response of Christian Europe to the impending disaster. As we are all destined to discover in our own moments of peril, true allies are always few and far between. And so it was then---the defense of Europe rested entirely on the shoulders of two men, Pope Pius V and Don John of Austria who alone, among the leaders of Europe, recognized the danger that was bearing down on them.

Gilbert Keith Chesterton, an English journalist in the ear-ly 1900's, was captivated by the immense significance of the sea battle which transpired between the Muslim and Christian forces on a Sunday in October in the Bay of Lepanto in 1571. A columnist for the London *Daily News,* Chesterton was well known for his defense of the Catholic Church, both historically and doctrinally.

TWO EPIC CHESTERTON POEMS

Valued for his erudition and wisdom, Chesterton was also well-loved for his kindly humor and entertaining style. Although mainly a prose writer, Chesterton also wrote poetry. One of his most successful literary efforts was *The Ballad of the White Horse,* an epic poem published in 1911, when Chesterton was 38.

Albertus Magnus

The *Ballad* commemorated another pivotal event in the history of Christendom, this time the defeat of the invading Viking forces by the beleaguered English king, Alfred the Great. Chesterton was convinced that if it hadn't been for Alfred, the just-emerging English culture in the 9th century would have been crushed by a barbarian tide that would have set England and perhaps all of Christian Europe back a few centuries.

For Chesterton, these two poems were a way to illustrate and magnify a theme that was of the utmost urgency to him: the need for brave souls to come forward in the defense of Christendom when it is attacked. Attack may come in different forms, but there will always be enemies of Christian civilization. There will also always be those who neglect their duties and by whose lack of vigilance our safety becomes threatened. Heroes come from unlikely places, and more often than not it is the ones the world looks down upon who will secure the victory.

Although there are parallels between the themes of *Lepanto* and *The Ballad of the White Horse,* they differ dramatically in form, length and tone, demonstrating Chesterton's prodigious versatility of expression.

READING LEPANTO

Before you begin reading *Lepanto,* look quickly through your text. If you will notice, the poem itself is on the grey-edged pages, which is only a small fraction of the book. What is the rest of the book?

Following the poem are several indispensable pages of notes. *Lepanto* is full of obscure allusions, for example, "Mahoud," "Azrael," "Ariel," and the "shadow of the Valois." Chesterton's audience in pre-World War Europe was much better-educated than the average modern reader and was familiar with most of Chesterton's references.

After the notes is a *Commentary* consisting of four brief essays which are also essential to understanding the poem: a historical background, an account of the battle from a military perspective, a discussion of the historical consequences of the battle and an entertaining discussion of the literary merits of the poem and interesting details about the author.

There are two essays at the back of the book. The first briefly explains different aspects of the poem. The second is an amusing piece of speculation on how history may have changed if Don John of Austria had kidnaped and married Mary, Queen of Scots! Be sure to read these on your own.

Before going on with our reading, be aware that there is an Answer Key in the Teacher's Guide which you should feel free to consult if you are having trouble with any of the questions.

Let's get started with our study of the battle of Lepanto by reading **"The Background,"** by Brendan Reyes, p. 51-57.

QUESTIONS

Take some time to look at the map on the right. Notice how the Ottoman Empire (the shaded area) was encroaching on the eastern borders of Europe and was fast approaching Spain's borders. After you have read the essay, answer the following questions.

1. Discuss how Europe in the middle of the sixteenth century was "diseased and divided," noting in particular the situation in each of these countries:

   a. Italy

   b. Spain

   c. France

   d. England

   e. Germany

2. How was the situation different in the Turkish Ottoman Empire?

3. What happened on the island of Cyprus? What was the significance of this horrifying event for Italy? *(Locate Famagusta on the map.)*

4. Who was the only leader in Europe to perceive the danger?

5. What was his response to the threat of Moslem attack?

Week 1, Day 2

Read **"The Battle,"** on p. 39-69 by Colonel Melvin Kriesel. This will give you an in-depth look at how this crucial naval battle was fought. The Janissaries are mentioned on p. 60 of the text. They were former Christians who had been conscripted into the Turkish army. After reading the essay, answer the questions below.

Janissaries

QUESTIONS

1. Who was the admiral of the Holy League? Describe the fleet he commanded.

2. What was the "Red Apple?" Why did the Turks want it?

3. Who was the commander of the Ottoman fleet? Describe his fleet and its unique battle-arrangement.

4. How did the Holy League's men prepare themselves for battle?

5. What was the miracle that occurred?

6. What were the three "surprises" the Christians sprang on the unsuspecting Turks?

7. How did Uluch Ali almost manage to turn the battle back in the Turks' favor at the last minute?

8. Describe the losses incurred by both sides.

9. Explain how Lepanto was a victory for the Holy League.

10. On what date was the battle of Lepanto fought?

After the battle at Lepanto, the people of Venice credited Our Lady of the Rosary (right) with their success. They publicly recorded he following declaration: "Neither strength, nor arms, nor leaders, but the Rosary of Our Lady made us the victors."

In addition, Pope Pius V ordered that every year there should be celebrated a feast in honor of Our Lady of Victory, to commemorate the great victory. Later, Pope Gregory XIII changed the name of the feast to Our Lady of the Rosary and ordered it to be celebrated on the date of the victory itself, the first Sunday of October. Recently, the date was fixed for October 7.

Read "The Aftermath," by William Cinfici on p. 71-75 which describes the immediate effect this great clash between Islam and Christian Europe had then and how the consequences of the Battle of Lepanto linger to this day. Answer the questions below.

QUESTIONS

1. Who was "the sick man of Europe?" Why was this country called this?

2. List the consequences of Lepanto remaining today in the Middle East.

3. What lasting feeling did the Christian victory at Lepanto leave among the followers of Islam?

4. In the author's opinion, what does Islam need in order to rise again?

5. What, strangely enough, happened to Christian Europe after Lepanto?

6. What is the "greatest legacy" of Lepanto? How did Lepanto shape our response as Catholics to dangerous times and situations? Who has historically come to our aid when we are most at peril?

Week 1, Day 4

The last essay you will read is "The Poem," by Dale Ahlquist, which will give you an excellent introduction to the poem and its author. Read p. 77-88 and answer the five questions below.

QUESTIONS

1. What inspired Chesterton to write *Lepanto*?

2. When was *Lepanto* written and published?

3. Why is this poem neglected today, in the author's opinion?

4. Explain why the battle of Lepanto was primarily a spiritual battle.

5. Does the poem paint a too-rosy picture of Catholics? Explain your answer.

Week 2, Day 1

You are now ready to begin reading the poem itself. Read the poem which is located on the gray-edged pages, taking time to enjoy this thrilling poem.

Week 2, Day 2
STRUCTURE AND POETIC ELEMENTS

Today we begin an analysis of the poem. Refer back to the text of the poem to answer the questions.

1. How many stanzas are in the poem?

2. Are all the stanzas of equal length?

3. Notice how stanzas 2,4,5,6, and 7 end. How is this different from the way stanzas 1, 3, and 8 end?

As you have probably noticed, stanzas 2, 4, 5, 6, and 7 end with a *refrain*. Chesterton uses other poetic elements throughout the poem to bind the verses together and to make it a harmonious whole. Look at some of these uses of repetition, called *poetic devices,* that he employs.

POETIC DEVICES

The examples of poetic devices on the next page are all taken from Chesterton's other famous poem, *The Ballad of the White Horse*. While *Lepanto* achieves its excitement primarily through the ingenious use of meter, the *Ballad*'s greatest art lies in its sumptuous blending of sounds. Let's look at the six most common devices used in his poetry.

alliteration: the repetition of initial consonant or vowel sounds.

"the **t**all **t**rees of Britain **we w**orshiped and **we**re **w**ise." *Initial consonants t and w are repeated.*

"When **A**lfred came to **A**thelney" *The short vowel sound a is repeated.*

assonance: the repetition of middle vowel sounds.

"white d**aw**n cr**aw**led through the wood" *The aw sound is repeated.*

"to gr**o**w **o**ld c**o**wed in a cr**o**wded land" *The long o sound is repeated. (The repetition of the ending consonant d is an example of consonance.)*

consonance: The repetition of middle or ending consonant sounds.

"Then bur**st**ing all and bla**st**ing came Chri**st**endom like death." *The medial consonant sound of st is repeated.*

"Ol**d** he was, but his locks were re**d**, yet he was sa**d** at boar**d** and be**d**." *The ending consonant d is repeated.*

Chesterton uses these three devices liberally in his poetry and in his prose writing. He will often combine all three in one passage. Let's take another striking illustration, this time a whole stanza from the *Ballad*:

> "**F**ollow a **l**ight tha**t l**eaps and spins
> **F**ollow the **f**ire un**f**ur**l**ed.
> **F**or **r**iseth up against **r**ealm and **r**od,
> A thing **f**or**g**o**t**ten, a thing down**t**rod,
> The **l**ast **l**os**t** giant, even God,
> Is **r**isen again**st** the wor**ld**."

The beginning consonants **f**, **l**, and **r** are repeated throughout, examples of *alliteration*. The same consonants **l** and **r** are also repeated in the middle of words which is an example of *consonance*. The consonants **t** and **d** are repeated at the end of words which are examples of *consonance*. Finally, the short vowel sound **o** is repeated throughout (f**o**llow, r**o**d, f**o**rgotten, downtr**o**d. l**o**st, G**o**d), an example of *assonance*.

In this passage Chesterton deftly manages to weave the audible effects in a tapestry of sounds and rhythm much the same way an artist will subtly use the same color tints in a painting to draw the whole together. In addition to these devices, Chesterton frequently uses three figures of speech, *simile, metaphor* and *personification*, in his poetry.

simile: the comparison of two unlike things with the use of *like* or *as*.

"Horses <u>like</u> horns of nightmare/Neigh horribly and long." *The neighing of horses is compared to the blowing of horns in a nightmare.*

"<u>as</u> evil cherubs rise, with little wings and lantern eyes." *Here owls flying in the woods as King Alfred passes are compared to "evil cherubs."*

Notice how the entire beginnning sound is repeated in this passage: **hor** (**hor**ses, **hor**ns, **hor**ribly). *Other examples of this are* "the **kin**sman of the **kin**g," "past **pur**ple forest and **pearl**ed foam" *and* "**har**dened his **heart**." *These are combinations of alliteration and assonance.*

metaphor: the comparison of two unlike things without like or as.

"God is a great gray servant," or "the tower that is the head of man." *In the first, God is identified as a servant, and in the second a man's head is identified as a tower. Metaphors are more direct than similes. An object is described as **being** something else.*

personification: an object is described as having human characteristics.

"Pride juggles with her toppling towers." *Here an abstract idea, pride, is described as a person juggling.*
"the sun's last smile." *The sun, an inanimate object, is describe as a smiling person.*

POETIC DEVICES IN LEPANTO

PRACTICE
On the line to the left of each quote, write the name of the device which is illustrated.

assonance   consonance   alliteration   simile   metaphor   personification

_____ 1. "**Boo**ms away past Italy the r**u**mor of his raid."

_____ 2. "He holds a crystal phial that has colors like the moon."

_____ 3. "We have **s**et the **s**eal of **S**olomon on all things under **s**un."

_____ 4. "and sift the red and silver sands lest bone of saint abide"

_____ 5. "where God *sits*"

_____ 6. "And his voice through all the garden is a thunder sent to bring"

RHYME SCHEME AND METER

Two important elements in the poem, *rhyme scheme* and *meter,* merit consideration. **Rhyme scheme** identifies the rhyming pattern in a stanza. The first rhyming word at the end of a line is known as A. In the following stanza, the first rhyming word is *sun.* All words rhyming with *sun* are also marked as A. The next rhyme is *feared,* and this is marked as B. All words rhyming with *feared* are marked as B. The next rhyme is *lips,* which is marked C. *Ships* is also marked C, and so on. Finish marking the rhyme scheme of this passage.

Selim II
Sultan of Constantinople

10   **White founts falling in the courts of the sun,**   A

15   **And the Soldan of Byzantium is smiling as they run.**   A

       There is laughter like the fountains in that face of all men feared.

       It stirs the forest darkness, the darkness of his beard.

       It curls the blood-red crescent, the crescent of his lips,

       For the inmost sea of all the earth is shaken with his ships.

       They have dared the white republics up the capes of Italy,

       They have dashed the Adriatic round the Lion of the Sea.

      The rhyme scheme of this passage should be **AABBCCDD**. The poem is composed of pairs of two rhyming lines. However, not all lines are of equal length. Some lines contain more syllables. Count the number of syllables in each of the lines above and mark it to the left of each line. The first two lines are done for you.

      Lines 7 and 8 have the same number of syllables and the same *meter* which will be discussed below. They also have the same, or *parallel,* sentence structure: *they have dared . . . they have dashed.* This is known as a *couplet.* Obviously if Chesterton had written the whole poem in couplets like this it would have been robotic and monotonous. He varies the length of the lines and the *rhythm* of the lines to provide auditory and visual interest to the reader.

      The *meter,* or pattern of beats which is found in every line, is an important element of Chesterton's poetry. Chesterton's masterful use of *meter* makes *Lepanto* an auditory and sensory delight. Meter invests the lines with a living, breathing quality and helps paint the various scenes in our minds. For instance, the staccato pounding of the refrain is like a barrage of cannon-shots. In contrast, the murmuring, chanting style of lines 48-54 in the fourth stanza has an eerie, hypnotizing effect.

      In another *couplet,* lines 11 and 12 in the first stanza, the pattern of beats or *meter* is the same in as it was in lines 7 and 8. The beats in each line are composed of *stressed* and *unstressed* syllables. There are two, three or four beats in a section, called a *foot.* Each line below has four sections or *feet.* Each *foot* is divided from the other by a vertical line.

      The cold queen of England is looking in the glass;

      The shadow of the Valois is yawning at the Mass;

      Observe carefully on the next page how these two lines are *scanned,* the process in which each syllable is marked as stressed or unstressed.

        The *unstressed* or *weak,* syllables are marked by this symbol: ◡

        The *stressed* or *strong,* syllables are marked with this symbol: ╱

˘ / ˘ ˘ / ˘ ˘ / ˘ ˘ ˘ /

The cold / queen of Eng / land is look / ing in the glass. ***(iambic/anapestic/anapestic/anapestic)***

˘ / ˘ ˘ ˘ / ˘ ˘ / ˘ ˘ ˘ /

The sha / dow of the Val / ois is yawn / ing at the Mass. ***(iambic/anapestic/anapestic/anapestic)***

IAMBIC In the first line the first foot is scanned ˘ / which is an *unstressed* (or weak) syllable followed by a *stressed* (or strong) syllable. This meter is known as **iambic**, and is used as a marching or martial rhythm.

ANAPESTIC The next three feet in the first line are scanned as ˘ ˘ / or ˘ ˘ ˘ / which is two or three unstressed syllables followed by a stressed syllable. This meter is known as **anapestic** and is lighter in feel than the **iambic,** and is considered a dancing rhythm. Both meters are *rising* patterns, meaning that the voice starts low and *rises up* on the stressed syllable.

The second line follows the same pattern: one iambic foot followed by three anapestic feet. In this poem Chesterton uses a combination of meters in many of the lines. However, every line except the refrain consists of four feet. If you will notice, *every line in the poem (excluding the refrain) has four strong beats with a varying number of weak beats in between.* As you read the poem, listen for those four strong beats in every line. They provide a subtle underpinning for the entire poem and give it consistency, much like a 4/4 tempo gives unity to a piece of music.

DACTYLIC Chesterton uses two other metric patterns in *Lepanto.* The next one considered is the **dactylic,** which is a *falling* pattern, meaning that it starts high, (or stressed) and ends on a lower tone. An example of this is in the refrain at the end of the second stanza (lines 32-35):

/ ˘ ˘ / ˘ ˘

Love light of / Spain–hurrah! ***(dactylic/dactylic)***

/ ˘ ˘ / ˘ ˘

Death-light of / Africa! ***(dactylic/dactylic)***

/ ˘ ˘ / ˘ ˘

Don John of / Austria ***(dactylic/dactylic)***

˘ / ˘ / ˘ /

Is rid /ing to / the sea. ***(iambic/iambic/iambic)***

In the refrain, there are three lines of two feet each, followed by a fourth line of three feet in iambic meter. The meter of the first three lines is **dactylic,** a stressed syllable followed by two or three unstressed syllables: / ˘ ˘. This is, incidentally, an abrupt change from the lines before it in the stanza which followed a mostly rising pattern.

SPONDEE The last meter we will discuss is Chesterton's creative use of the **spondee** which is a foot composed of two stressed syllables together / /. Chesterton combines the spondee with other meters in the same line to remarkable effect. There are several lines in the poem which follow this pattern: **spondee / dactyl / iamb / spondee**. If it is scanned it looks like this: / / | / / ˘ | ˘ ˘ / | / / . This arrangement allows the line to begin with three strong beats, have three weak beats in the middle and then end with three strong beats. They are used at the beginning of the first and second stanzas and at other dramatic moments in the poem.
This pattern is used in several lines throughout the poem.

Dim drums / throbbing in / the hills / half heard.
(spondee)   *(dactyl)*   *(iamb)*   *(spondee)*

PRACTICE

In order to give you some practice with the four types of meter we have discussed, **scan** or mark with ′ ◡ all the beats below and **match** the following patterns with each line of verse. To help you, the scanning pattern is given below for each line. Write the number of the answer on the line to the right.

1) **iambic in all four feet** ◡ ′ / ◡ ′ / ◡ ′ / ◡ ′
2) **anapestic in all four feet** ◡ ◡ ′ / ◡ ◡ ′/ ◡ ◡ ′ / ◡ ◡ ′
3) **iambic (1) / anapestic (3)** ◡ ′ / ◡ ◡ ′/ ◡ ◡ ′/ ◡ ◡ ′
4) **dactylic (3) / iambic (1)** ′ ◡ ◡ / ′ ◡ ◡ / ′ ◡ ◡/ ◡ ′
5) **spondee/dactyl/iamb/spondee** ′ ′ / ′ ◡ ◡/ ◡ ′ / ′ ′

_____ 1. **Don John / laughing in / the brave / beard curled.**

_____ 2. **Like a race / in sunken ci / ties, like a na / tion in the mines.**

_____ 3. **Comes up / along / a wind / ing road / the noise / of the / Crusade.**

_____ 4. **The voice / that shook our pa / laces four hun / dred years ago.**

_____ 5. **Crying with the / trumpet, the / trumpet of / his lips.**

Week 2, Day 3
STANZA I

A closer look at this wonderful poem ensues, employing the excellent endnotes beginning on p. 18. Read the notes for Stanza 1 (Lines 1-14) on p. 18-22 and re-read the first stanza again. The notes should give a much clearer picture of the scenes Chesterton is carefully constructing. After reading the stanza answer the questions. The literal and symbolic meanings will be examined along with Chesterton's skillful use of language.

QUESTIONS
1. Where are we when the poem begins?

2. Describe the Soldan of Byzantium in your own words.

3. Who is the "cold queen" and the "shadow of the Valois?"

4. What is the response of England and France to the Pope's call for help?

5. Scan with ⌣ and ´ the following lines and answer the questions about each:

a) **There is laugh / ter like the foun / tains in that face / of all men feared.**

   1. What type of meter is used in this line?

   2. What are the two alliterations in this line? Underline them.

   3. What is the *simile*? What two things are being compared?

b) **They have dared / the white repub / lics up the capes / of Italy.**

   They have dashed / the Adria / tic round the Li / on of the Sea.

Explain how these two lines are the same in the following ways:

   rhyme:

   meter:

   parallel sentence structure:

c) **White founts / falling in the / courts of / the sun.**

   1. Describe the meter.

   2. Tell about any poetic devices.

STANZA II

In this stanza attention is focused on one of the heroes of Christendom, Don John of Austria. Now the leaders of the two great forces which are being rapidly and inexorably drawn together have been introduced. Read the notes on p. 22-24 first and then read stanza 2 (Lines 15-35) on p. 11-12, and answer the questions below.

Crusader receiving Holy Communion before leaving for the Holy Land

QUESTIONS

1. Describe the setting as this stanza begins.

2. There are descriptions of Don John of Austria in the following three lines of the poem. Write them below.

Line 16:

Line 18:

Line 19:

3. Scan Line 15, the first line of Stanza 2 and answer the questions.

Dim drums / throbbing in the hills / half heard.

a) What special pattern (see p.11) does this follow?

b) Why do you think this pattern is used here? What sound is Chesterton trying to imitate?

c) Tell about any alliterations you hear.

4. The **spondee/dactyl/iamb/spondee** pattern is used in three more lines in this stanza. Find and copy below.

a)
b)
c)

6. Notice that Lines 2-22 in this stanza have a *rising* pattern where the first syllable is not stressed. From line 23 on, however, there is a *falling* pattern so the first syllable of every line is stressed (except 26 and 28). What feeling is conveyed by this dramatic change in meter?

7. Scan the last four lines of Stanza 2, the *refrain*. The first line is scanned for you. Answer questions below.

´ ᴜ ᴜ ´ ᴜ ᴜ
Love light of / Spain hurrah!

Death light of / Africa!

Don John of / Austria

Is rid / ing to / the sea.

a) Is this a *rising* or *falling* pattern in the first three lines?
b) What meter is being used in the first three lines?
c) What meter is used in the fourth line?
d) What assonance is heard in the third line?

Week 2, Day 1

STANZA III

The confrontation shaping up between Islam and Christendom takes on a new and chilling dimension as Mahound conjures up supernatural forces of evil to come to the aid of his followers. Read the notes for this stanza on p. 24-27. Read the stanza, Lines 36-47, and answer the questions below.

QUESTIONS

1. How does the scene shift in this stanza?

A genie is summoned from his bottle.

2. Copy Line 37 and explain why it is in parentheses.

3. Identify the *assonances*, *alliterations* and *consonances* in these lines:

> **He moves a mighty turban on the timeless houri's knees.**
> **His turban that is woven from the sunset and the trees.**
> **He shakes the peacock gardens as he rises from his ease.**
> **And he strides among the tree-tops and is taller than the trees.**

> > **alliterations:**
> > **consonances:**
> > **assonances:**

4. Whom is Mahound summoning to his aid?

5. Give the rhyme scheme for this stanza.

Week 2, Day 2
STANZA IV

The gathering of evil forces continues and a closer look at the philosophical divide between Christian and Muslim is given. Read the endnotes for this stanza on p. 27-32 and then read Stanza 3 again, Lines 49-73. Answer the questions below.

QUESTIONS
1. Copy Lines 50 and 51.

2. What creatures are referred to in Lines 48-55 and what task are they given?

3. Scan the following three lines and answer questions on the next page.

> **It is he / that saith not Kis / met; it is he / that knows not Fate;**
> **It is Rich / ard, it is Ray / mond, it is God / frey in the gate!**
> **It is he / whose loss is laugh / ter when he counts / the wager worth.**

Richard the Lion-Hearted

a) What specific group of people is being described in each line? `

b) What does Mahound want to do to them?

c) Tell about the poetic devices.

4. Scan the four-line stanza below.

Sudden and / still—hurrah!

Bolt from I / beria!

Don John of / Austria

Is gone / by Al / calar.

Week 2, Day 3
STANZA V

Now St. Michael, the great defender of heaven and scourge of devils, enters the fray and sounds the alarm to France. Read the endnotes on p. 32-35 and then read the third stanza (Lines 74-91).

QUESTIONS

1. What country is referred to in Lines 74-79? What is its response to the war-alarms?

2. Copy Line 75. Explain what it means.

3. Copy Line 78 and 79. Answer the questions below

   a) Whom does this line refer to?

   b) What is he doing?

   c) Mark the poetic devices and tell about them briefly:

      alliteration:
      consonance:
      personification:

4. Study Lines 80-81 below and answer the questions.

> **The North is full of tangled things and texts and aching eyes**
> **And dead is all the innocence of anger and surprise.**

a) What country does this refer to?

b) Discuss what this means. *(Refer to the endnotes again if necessary.)*

c) Tell about poetic devices.

5. Copy Lines 82-84. Answer the question below.

What group of people is being targeted in each line?

6. Read the lines below. Note the scanning marks. Below the line, tell what pattern it is repeating.

> **Don John / calling through / the blast / and the / eclipse.**

PATTERN:

7. Scan the refrain and answer the questions below.

> **Trumpet that / sayeth ha!**
>
> **Domino / gloria!**
>
> **Don John of / Austria**
>
> **Is shout / ing to / the ships.**

a) What is Don John doing at this point?

b) What does *"Domino gloria"* mean?

Week 2, Day 4

STANZA VI

Here we are given a disconcerting glimpse of the Catholic monarchy in Spain. All is clearly not well with King Philip and his own sinister motives are hinted at here. Read the endnotes for this stanza on p. 35-38, then read the sixth stanza. (Lines 92-107). Answer the questions about this stanza below.

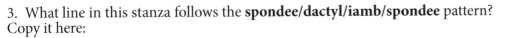
Philip II

QUESTIONS

1. What country and its monarch are being described in Lines 92-100?

2. What two similes does Chesterton use to describe the king's face?

    1)

    2)

3. What line in this stanza follows the **spondee/dactyl/iamb/spondee** pattern?
Copy it here:

4. Copy the four-line refrain here and answer the questions below:

    a) What has just happened aboard the Christian ships?

    b) How does the meter and language reflect the meaning of these lines?

Week 4, Day 1

STANZA VII

The tension mounts as the two enormous forces prepare to engage each other. Notice the contrast between the beginning and end of this stanza. It begins in stillness and solitude and ends in the bloody turmoil and din of battle. Read the endnotes for this stanza on p. 38-44. Re-read the stanza, Lines108-137. Answer the questions about this stanza on the next page.

QUESTIONS

1. Describe the scene as this stanza opens in your own words.

2. Copy Line 112 and explain what it means.

3. Read the lines below and circle the letter of the group of adjectives below that best describes the tone of these lines and of Lines 113-126.

> **They are countless, voiceless, helpless as those fallen or fleeing on**
> **Before the high Kings' horses in the granite of Babylon.**

a) lazy, sleepy, murmuring
b) striking, thunderous, thrilling
c) chanting, droning, hypnotic

4. At what line does a sudden, dramatic change occur? **This is the climax!** Write it here.

5. Scan the following lines which vividly describe the high point of the battle.

> **Don John / pounding from the / slaug hter-paint / ed poop.**
>
> **Purpling all the / ocean like a / bloody pi / rate's sloop.**
>
> **Scarlet running / over on the / silvers and / the golds.**
>
> **Breaking of the / hatches up and / bursting of / the holds.**
>
> **Thronging of the / thousands up that / labor un / der sea.**
>
> **White for bliss and / blind for sun and / stunned for lib / erty.**

a) What meter is most used in all the lines except the first?

b) Which line is **spondee/dactyl/dactyl/iamb**?

c) What part of speech are the underlined words?

d) Why did Chesterton use this type of verb throughout this passage?

e) Excluding the first line, how many *strong (stressed) beats* are in each line?

6. Describe the effect of this important passage on you.

7. Does the poem sustain the dramatic tone of this passage to the end or does it subside? (*Note that Chesterton has created the tone of this poem through his use of meter. Does the intense, driving meter of the climax continue to the end of the poem?*)

8. Copy down the last refrain and answer the two questions below.

       a) What does *Vivat Hispania* mean?

       b) Explain what has just happened.

Week 4, Day 2
STANZA VIII

    As the excitement and noise of battle recedes, we meet the last player in the saga of Lepanto, Miguel Cervantes. Despite being acclaimed a hero at Lepanto, he returns home to Spain and spends many years in difficulty and poverty. Disillusioned and embittered, he writes *Don Quixote*, where he calls into question the chivalric ideals and romantic spirit of the Middle Ages. The reader is left to decide which is the correct version of Don John: Was he just a quaint, foolish knight on an impossible quest for glory, or was he a brave and generous man who resisted the pull towards self-preservation and autonomy that was paralyzing Europe then and who believed that all Christians should pull together to protect Europe?

    Read the endnotes on p. 44-47 and then read the stanza, Lines 138-143. Answer the questions below when you are finished reading.

QUESTIONS

1. Who is Cervantes and what is his significance here? (*Read the last paragraph of Chesterton's essay, "The True Romance" for a further look at Cervantes.*)

2. How does Cervantes see Don John? Write the phrase he uses to describe Don John in Line 141.

3. How are the beginning and end of the poem alike?

4. Describe your mood as the poem ends.

Now that you have completed your study of *Lepanto*, be sure to re-visit it from time to time. Good poetry, you will find, has a unique power to stir the soul and the senses, and this poem is one of the very best ever written. It is easy to understand why the soldiers were "shouting it in the trenches" during World War I!

This poem, in just a few stanzas, explores the best and the worst in men---the constant struggle of good versus evil. It celebrates the triumph of resolution and courage over indifference and corruption, of solidarity and Christian brotherhood over independence and isolation, and, most importantly, of prayer and hope over the forces of destruction and darkness.

Lepanto is the incredible story of two most unlikely heroes: a 24-year old illegitimate prince and a frail old Pope who, together with a small force of men, confront head-on, rosaries in hand, and trust in God in their hearts, the powerful, experienced Turkish navy which vastly outnumbered them in ships and men.

Miraculously, with God's grace and the Blessed Mother's help, they soundly defeat the Turks and return in triumph, the bells of Christendom ringing out in gratitude to greet them:

Vivat Hispania!
Domino gloria!
Don John of Austria
Has set his people free!

FINAL NOTES

If your Home Instructor plans to give you the test on *Lepanto,* spend some time looking over the Review Questions on the next page.

After you have finished the test there is an optional short book included on St. Pius V that will give you an excellent understanding of this time period as well as a chance to learn more about this most fascinating man who was able to accomplish an astonishing amount in his six-year reign as Pope.

He was not only responsible for saving Europe from a Turkish invasion, he also carried out the reforms of the Council of Trent, issued the Roman Missal, the Breviary and the Catechism of Trent. If that were not enough, he successfully conducted several important transactions with European heads of state during this time. Above all, Pope Pius V was a man of great personal holiness whose concern for the spiritual and temporal welfare of all those in his care was extraordinary.

For those going further in their study of Lepanto, begin reading *St. Pius V* by Prof. Robin Anderson.

Our Lady of Victory, pray for us.
Our Lady of the Rosary, pray for us.

REVIEW QUESTIONS

1. Review the work you have done on the historical background of the poem. Know the following:

    a) the events leading up to the battle

    b) the actual course of the battle

    c) the commanders of both sides

    d) the consequences of the battle

2. Be able to identify the following characters:

    a) Holy League

    b) Pope Pius V

    c) Don John of Austria

    d) Selim II

    e) King Philip II of Spain

3. Review the poetic terms discussed:

    a) the six poetic devices

    b) refrain

    c) rhyme scheme

    d) four types of meter

    e) the metrical patterns used in the poem

4. Know the sequence of the poem.

5. What is the climax of the poem?

6. What is the end of the poem?

7. How did *Lepanto* come to be written?

8. What other great poem did Chesterton write?

9. What was the "sick man of Europe?"

10. Explain why Don John was considered a hero.

DISCUSSION QUESTIONS FOR PIUS V, BY ROBIN ANDERSON

CHAPTER 1, "FROM SHEPHERD BOY TO POPE"

1. What was Michael Ghislieri's family background?

Pope St. Pius V

2. What important office did he hold before he was elected Pope?

3. What was his initial response *after* being elected Pope?

CHAPTER 2, "SOVEREIGN PONTIFF AND TEMPORAL REFORM"

1. What much-needed reforms did he bring to the city of Rome?

2. What was this Pope's attitude toward the poor and unfortunate?

CHAPTER 3, "SPIRITUAL REFORM"

1. What area of the Church did he seek to reform first after his own household?

2. Whom did he declare a Doctor of the Church?

3. What result did his efforts to increase the faith and piety of the Church bring about?

CHAPTER 4, "PROTESTANTISM AND EUROPEAN DIPLOMACY"

1. How did Pius' unworldly perspective and spiritual detachment actually aid his efforts to work with the European rulers?

3. What did his Bull *Regnans in excelsis* declare?

CHAPTER 5, "LEPANTO: THE HOLY ALLIANCE AGAINST THE TURKS"

1. How does this account of Philip II of Spain differ from Chesterton's view of that monarch?

2. What event was the deciding factor in the Holy League's decision to fight and not turn back?

3. What title did Pope Pius add to the Litany of Loreto to honor Our Lady for her help in their success?

CHAPTER 6, "THE ROMAN CATECHISM, BREVIARY AND MISSAL"

1. Why was the Council of Trent so effective in bringing about spiritual reform in the Church?

2. What was the aim of the Council of Trent in revising the *Roman Missal*?

3. Was the *Missal* a new invention?

4. What was the reaction of priests and laity to Pius V's revision and legislation of the *Roman Missal?*

CHAPTER 7, "LAST DAYS AND DEATH"

1. What miracle occurred which prevented him from being poisoned?

2. What were reported to be his final words?

CHAPTER 8, "MIRACLES, BEATIFICATION, AND CANONIZATION"

1. Where do Pope Pius' remains rest now?

2. When was he canonized and by whom?

TEST AND ANSWER KEY

LEPANTO TEST

A. IDENTIFICATION Identify whom is being described in each line. One character has two sentences describing him.

King Philip II   St. Michael   Christian galley slave   Don John of Austria

Pope St. Pius V   Mahound   Selim II   Devils   Miguel Cervantes

_____ 1. "They swell in sapphire smoke out of the blue cracks of the ground."

_____ 2. "He strides among the tree-tops and is taller than the trees."

_____ 3. "The last and lingering troubadour to whom the bird has sung."

_____ 4. "He sees as in a mirror on the monstrous twilight sea."

_____ 5. "He finds his God forgotten, and he seeks no more a sign."

_____ 6. "He smiles, but not as Sultans smile, and settles back the blade."

_____ 7. "He shakes his lance of iron and he claps his wings of stone."

_____ 8. "He holds a crystal phial that has colors like the moon."

_____ 9. "The Lord upon the Golden Horn is laughing in the sun."

_____ 10. "A lean and foolish knight forever rides in vain."

B. IDENTIFICATION Identify which of the six poetic devices is being used in each line. The number in parentheses indicates how times that device is demonstrated in the examples.

alliteration (2)   **consonance** (1)   **assonance**(2)
simile (2)   **metaphor** (1)   **personification** (2)

_____ 1. "The Lord upon the Golden Horn is laughing in the sun."

_____ 2. "Strong gongs groaning as the guns boom far."

_____ 3. "There is laughter like the fountains"

_____ 4. "He touches, and it tingles, and he trembles very soon."

_____ 5. "Crying with the trumpet, the trumpet of his lips."

_____ 6. "Spurning of his stirrups like the thrones of all the world."

TEST (continued)

_____ 7. "Thronging of the thousands up that labour under sea."

_____ 8. "Like a race in sunken cities, like a nation in the mines."

_____ 9. "He heard drums groaning."

_____ 10. "Trumpet that sayeth ha!"

C. SCANNING Scan each of the lines and tell which metrical pattern described below is used.

1. "Stiff flags / straining in / the night / blasts cold."
PATTERN:

2. "White for bliss and / blind for sun and / stunned for li / berty."
PATTERN:

3. "The North / is full / of tan / gled things / and texts / and ach / ing eyes."
PATTERN:

4. "It is Rich / ard; it is Ray / mond; it is God / frey in / the gate!"
PATTERN:

5. "For that / which was our trou / ble comes again / out of the west."
PATTERN:

METRICAL PATTERNS
A. dactyl / dactyl / dactyl / iamb
B. spondee / dactyl / iamb / spondee
C. anapest / anapest / anapest / iamb
D. iamb / iamb / iamb / iamb
E. iamb / anapest / anapest / anapest

TEST (continued)

D. SHORT ANSWER   Give a brief answer for each.

1. What event precipitated the Battle of Lepanto?

2. Name the three European monarchs described in the poem.

3. Who was the Pope during this crucial time and what role did he play?

4. What was the Holy League?

5. What was the "Red Apple?"

6. Give the date and location of the Battle.

7. What was the miracle that occurred during the battle?

8. What was the "sick man of Europe?"

9. What book did Cervantes write after he returned from Lepanto?

10. What other famous poem did Chesterton publish in the same year as *Lepanto*?

E. LITERARY ANALYSIS Scan the following lines and answer the questions below.

Gun upon / gun, ha! ha!

Gun upon / gun, hurrah!

Don John of / Austria

Has loosed / the can / nonade.

> a. What meter is used in the first three lines?

> b. What meter is used in the last line?

> c. What is this four-line passage called?

> d. How many strong beats in the first three line of this passage?

> e. How many strong beats are in all the other lines of the poem?

> f. Explain what has just happened in the battle and how Chesterton conveys the scene and its sound effects through his use of language and meter.

TEST (continued)

F. ESSAYS In your best writing technique, answer the following in 3-4 paragraphs. Remember to give an introduction and a conclusion.

1. Describe Don John of Austria in your own words. What was his role in the Battle of Lepanto? How should we strive to be like him in our own lives?

2. What is the historical and spiritual significance of the Battle of Lepanto?

ANSWER KEY

"THE BACKGROUND" (p. 3-4)

1. Europe was "diseased and divided" because of the interior conflicts in key European countries and division between countries.

a) Italy, as a result of the Renaissance and Machiavellian politics, was mostly concerned with maintaining and expanding her commercial interests.

b) King Philip had his hands full trying to maintain control over the Spanish mainland and territories. In addition, he had to keep the large Muslim population in Spain in check.

c) France was divided by internal religious conflict. The aristocracy saw in the civil disturbances the chance to challenge the power of the French monarchy.

d) In England, Queen Elizabeth was primarily concerned with building up the new Church of England and with reducing the pockets of resistance to her new religion.

e) The Emperor was preoccupied with settling disputes between Catholic and Protestant states after the Peace of Augsburg in 1555.

2. The Ottoman Empire was strong and unified. Under Suleiman the Magnificent, it was extended to include most of the northern coast of Africa and all along the Mediterranean coast to the Balkans and Hungary. Suleiman's son and successor, Selim II, like all Sultans, was expected to add more states to the Empire. He turned his attention to Cyprus, planning to go from there to Italy.

3. Selim's forces took over Nicosia, the capital, and massacred all 20,000 of its inhabitants. Then they took the port city of Famagusta, skinning Famagusta's governor alive. From there, the Turks began raiding the Venetian islands in the Adriatic.

4. Pope Pius V was greatly concerned with both the threat of Muslim invasion and conquest of Europe and the threat of Protestantism dividing Europe so it could not present a unified front against the Turks.

5. Because the governments of Spain and Italy, the countries most threatened by Muslim attack, were ignoring the problem, the Pope worked to form the Holy League, an alliance of individuals from Venice, Spain and the Papal States.

"THE BATTLE" (p. 4-5)

1. Don John of Austria, the illegitimate son of Emperor Charles V and half-brother of Philip II of Spain, was recommended by Pope Pius to lead the Christian fleet– the largest Christian naval force ever assembled: 208 war galleys and 76 smaller ships. There were 30,000 soldiers and another 50,000 prisoners and slaves manning the oars.

2. Rome was the Red Apple because it was full of treasure and was the political center of Europe. If Rome fell, all of Europe would soon fall, too.

3. Muezzinzade Ali Pasha commanded 300 galleys and 80 gunships carrying over 100,000 men. Ali Pasha had his fleet arranged in a giant crescent with the flagship, the *Sultana*, in the center, the Sultan's own huge green banner with "Allah" embroidered on it 28,900 times in gold boldly displayed from the mast.

4. The priests on deck went about with raised crucifixes, blessing the men and hearing their last confessions. Every man had a rosary and thousands of Christians at home and the Pope were praying the rosary for their success.

"THE BATTLE" (p. 4-5) (cont.)

5. The wind, which had been blowing in the Turk's favor, suddenly dropped and shifted direction to blow against the Turkish fleet. This freed up thousands of Christians from the galleys of the Christians to fight in the battle. See the interesting story of Our Lady of Guadalupe's involvement in the battle on the bottom of p. 46 in the text.

6. The three surprises of the Christian forces were
1) six war galleys, heavily armed with cannons, fired into and crippled the advancing Turkish ships.
2) the removal of the iron rams on the galleys allowed cannon fire for the first time in battle to hit the enemy ships below their water lines, sinking many Turkish ships with a single volley.
3) the Janisseries' attempt to board the Christian ships was foiled when they were trapped in the boarding nets which Don John had ordered to be hung from stem to stern on his ships. Thousands were trapped and easily shot down by the soldiers on board the Christian ships.

7. His corsairs slipped through a gap in the line and began to attack the rear of the Christians's main line. They destroyed nearly all of the Maltese force before being stopped by reserve galleys led by Santa Cruz.

8. The Christians lost 7,000 men and 12 galleys. The Turks lost over 30,000 men and had only 13 galleys left at the end of the day.

9. The Christians captured over 300 ships and freed 15,000 Christian galley slaves from the Turkish ships. The huge losses on the Turkish side would take years to replace. The Turks' advance into Europe was effectively stopped.

10. The first Sunday of October, Oct. 7, 1571.

"THE AFTERMATH" (p. 6)

1. The "Sick Man of Europe" was Turkey. After Lepanto and the Turks's failed siege of Vienna in 1683, the Ottoman Empire began to lose territories. Other nations, starting with Greece, became independent. By World War I, nearly all of North Africa had been taken away, and after the war, the only part of the Empire left was Turkey.

2. The Ottoman Empire has been replaced with independent Arab states which are always in a state of conflict with each other and with other nations: Turkey vs. Greece, the struggle of Christians and Muslims in Yugoslavia, and, finally, the constant struggle in Palestine between Jordan and Israel.

3. They still feel defeated and cannot reconcile their defeat with their belief in Allah who is supposed to help them overcome the world. Because Islam was not able to defeat the West by conventional means, the most radical among them have resorted to terrorism.

4. If they are to rise again, Muslims need to unite under a leader who lead them in their struggle to take over the West. Many Muslims do not want a war of conquest, but the author believes that if enough of the most radical could join forces, they could become a most dangerous enemy again.

5. It collapsed because of the religious schism caused by Protestantism. Protestant influence has led to a general loss of faith even among Catholics in Europe coinciding with the rise of the merchant class over small independent producers which has led to a loss of freedom and autonomy. Europe still has a stronger military force than Islamic forces, but there is not much incentive among Europeans to fight another "holy war." European demographics have also changed drastically because of widespread generational birth control use.

Muslims in Europe, because they believe in having large families, have quickly caught up to the native Eu-ropean population and will someday outnumber them. The Muslims can hypothetically take over peacefully through sheer force of numbers.

6. The Christian victory at Lepanto inspired a great confidence and devotion to the Rosary. It has become for many Catholics the first spiritual line of defense against trouble. Many Catholics will carry a rosary with them or even in their car even though they are not regular Mass attendees since it has become an indispensable part of the Catholic identity. The Blessed Mother has always come to our aid and has come to warn us of impending disasters when we are most in danger. Again and again she has come to offer us the solution to our problems and the way to obtain peace: penance and prayer, especially the prayer of the Rosary. A few examples: Our Lady of Guadalupe converted millions of native Central Americans from their satanic religion and culture. In Poland in 1655, the country was in grave danger of being overrun by the Swedish Lutherans and being annexed to Sweden. They were betrayed by several Polish nobles, the King fled, but the common people rose up to defend their country. The King returned and dedicated himself and his nation to Our Lady of Czestochowa, as the "Queen of the Polish Crown." National unity was regained and they were able to throw off the aggressors. At La Salette, she warned of terrible punishments that would come if the people did not return to the practice of their religion. At Fatima, she warned us of the rise of Communism which has become the most destructive force in modern times and exhorted us to say the Rosary for peace and the conversion of Russia. The Communist threat is far from over, and it would be-hoove us greatly to take our Mother's advice more to heart.

"THE POEM" (p. 7)
1. Chesterton's friend, Fr. O'Connor, gave a speech on Lepanto which gave Chesterton the idea for his poem. He even wrote a few lines as he was listening to Fr. O' Connor speak.

2. It was written on Oct. 7, 1911 and published that week!

3. It is ignored because it is a defense of the Catholic Church, the Crusades and war, none of which are regarded with any favor by the educational elite even in most Catholic schools.

4. The Battle of Lepanto has a spiritual significance on many fronts. The spiritual apathy and indifference of the Catholic European leaders during the Crusades and after caused the threat of Islam to swell. The religious conflict in Europe between Protestants and Catholics prevented a sufficient force from being gathered to deal with the growing threat of conquest. Finally, the victory itself was clearly miraculous, the answer to the prayers of the Pope and the faithful.

5. Not at all. In fact it brings into focus the neglect, indifference and corruption of several key Catholic figures: Philip II of Spain, Charles IX of France and the Holy Roman Emperor in Germany.

"STRUCTURE AND POETIC ELEMENTS" (p. 7)
1. It has 8 stanzas.

2. No, several are very short while others are much longer.

3. The former end with a four-line refrain. The others do not have a refrain.

PRACTICE (p. 9-10)
1. **assonance:** the **oo** sound in *rumor* and *booms*. There is also an alliteration with rumor and raid. Booms is an onomatopoeia, a word that imitates the sound with which it is associated.

2. **simile:** the color of the phial is compared to the color of the moon. There is an assonance with ph**i**al and l**i**ke, the long **i** sound.

3. **alliteration:** the **s** sound in *set, seal, Solomon, sun.*

4. **consonance:** the **d** sound in *and, red, sands, and abide.*

5. **personification:** God, a spiritual Being, is described as a person sitting.

6. **metaphor:** Mahound's voice is compared to thunder.

PRACTICE (p. 12)
1. 5) **spondee/dactyl/iamb/spondee**

2. 2) **anapestic in all four feet**

3. 1) **iambic in all four feet**

4. 3) **iambic (1) / anapestic (3)**

5. 4) **dactyl (3)/ iambic (1)**

STANZA I (p. 13-15)
1. This scene opens in the Sultan Selim's courtyard somewhere in the Mediterranean.

2. Answers will vary.

3. Queen Elizabeth of England and King Charles IX of France.

4. The Queen offers no help at all. She is absorbed in her own world: **"looking in the glass."** Charles is totally indifferent to the Pope's concerns and to spiritual matters: **"yawning at the Mass."**

5.   a) **There is laugh / ter like the foun / tains in that face / of all men feared.**
        1. The meter is anapestic
        2. The alliterations are laughter, like and fountains, face, feared.
        3. The simile is **"laughter *like the fountains.*"**

   b) **They have dared / the white repub / lics up the capes / of Italy.**

   They have dashed / the Adria / tic round the Li / on of the Sea.

> rhyme: Italy and sea rhyme with each other.
>
> meter: both lines are anapestic in all four feet.
>
> parallel sentence structure: both lines have the same grammatical structure: Subject/helping verb/main verb/direct object/adverbial prepositional phrase/adjectival prepositional phrase.

       ´   ´   ´ ◡ ◡   ◡   ´ ◡   ◡ ´

c) **White founts / falling in the / courts of / the sun.**
   1. This is **spondee/dactyl/iamb/iamb**, a slight variation.
   2. The alliteration is **f**ounts, **f**alling.

STANZA II (p. 14-15)

1. The opening scene is set in the hills of Alpugarras where Don John of Austria has just finished putting down a Muslim uprising.

2.   Line 16: "**a crownless prince.**"

   Line 18: "**the last knight of Europe.**"

   Line 19: "**the last and lingering troubadour to whom the bird has sung.**"

    ´   ´   ´ ◡ ◡   ◡ ´   ´   ´

3. **Dim drums / throbbing in / the hills / half heard.**
   a) The rhythm is **spondee/dactyl/iamb/spondee**.
   b) The strong rhythmic pattern recalls drumbeats.
   c) There are alliterations with the consonants **d** and **h**.

4.   a) "**Strong gongs groaning as the guns boom far.**"
   b) "**Don John laughing in the brown beard curled.**"
   c) "**Stiff flags straining in the night-blasts cold.**"

5. "**Spurning of his stirrups like the thrones of all the world.**" This is a simile explaining how Don John had no use for his stirrups in the same way he had no interest in being a king.

6. There is an increasing sense of excitement as Don John begins his mission to free Europe from the threat of Islam.

       ´   ◡   ◡   ´ ◡ ◡

7.   **Death light of / Africa!**

       ´   ◡   ◡   ´ ◡ ◡

Don John of / Austria

      ◡ ´   ◡ ´   ◡ ´

Is rid / ing to / the sea.

a) The first three lines follow a *falling* pattern.
b) The first three lines are dactylic in both feet.
c) The fourth line is iambic.
d) assonance: the short **o** sound.

STANZA III (p. 15-16)
1. Muhammed is in his "paradise" in his afterlife.

2. This indicates what Don John is doing simultaneously with the rest of the poem. Two story lines are being spun out, like a movie or a novel which switches back and forth from the plot and the subplot. The lines in parentheses serve to increase the tension as the poem comes closer to the confrontation between the two great forces.

3. **alliterations:** the **m** and **t** sounds: **m**oves, **m**ighty; **t**urban, **t**imeless, **t**ree-tops, **t**aller
   consonances: the beginning **t** sound and in the middle and end of words: migh**t**y, **t**ha**t**, sunse**t**, s**t**rides
   assonances: the **ur** sound: t**ur**ban, ho**ur**i's; the **ee** sound: houri's, trees, peacock, he, ease, treetop, trees

4. Mahound is calling up various false gods and evil spirits.

5. **AABBCCDDEEED.**

STANZA IV (p. 16-17)
1. **They rise in green robes roaring from the green hells of the sea**
   Where fallen skies and evil hues and eyeless creatures be.

2. Lucifer and his fallen angels. Mahound tells them to destroy the relics of the saints and also to suppress the Christians so there will be an Islamic "peace."

3.
    ᵕ ᵕ ´   ᵕ   ᵕ ᵕ ´   ᵕ ᵕᵕ ´   ᵕ   ᵕ   ᵕ ´

    It is he / that saith not Kis / met; it is he / that knows not Fate;
    ᵕ ᵕ ´   ᵕ ᵕᵕ ´   ᵕ ᵕᵕ ´   ᵕ ᵕ ᵕ ´

    It is Rich / ard; it is Ray / mond, it is God / frey in the gate!
    ᵕ ᵕ ´   ᵕ   ᵕ ᵕ ´   ᵕ ᵕ   ᵕ ´   ᵕ ᵕ ᵕ ´

    It is he / whose loss is laugh / ter when he counts / the wager worth.

    a) The first line refers to the Christians who believe in free will and are not merely resigned to Fate. The second line refers to the leaders of the First and Third Crusades. The third line refers to the Christian martyrs.
    b) He wants to crush them and force them to submit to the "will" of Allah.
    c) **alliteration:** the letters **r, g, l,** and **w**: **R**ichard, **R**aymond, **G**odfrey, **g**ate, **l**oss, **l**aughter, **wh**ose, **w**hen, **w**ager. **w**orth
        assonance: long **a**: saith, Fate, Raymond, gate, wager; short **i**: it, is, Kismet, Richard, in
        consonance: the letter **t**: it, Kismet, that, Fate, gate, laughter, counts

4.
      ´ ᵕ ᵕ   ´ ᵕ ᵕ
    Sudden and / still—hurrah!

      ´   ᵕ ᵕ ´ᵕ ᵕ
    Bolt from I / beria!
      ´   ᵕ ᵕ ´ᵕ ᵕ
    Don John of / Austria

      ᵕ ´ ᵕ ´ ᵕ ´
    Is gone / by Al / calar.

STANZA V (p. 17-18)
1. The country referred to is France. It ignores the Pope's call.

2. **"Don John is girt and going forth."** Don John sets out on his journey to Lepanto, fully armed and going forth to do battle.

3. **He shakes his lance of iron and claps his wings of stone.**
   The noise is gone through Normandy; the noise is gone alone.
The letter **n** is found in both **alliteration** and **consonance** in this passage: la**n**ce, iro**n**, wi**n**gs, sto**n**e, **n**oise, go**n**e, **N**ormandy, alo**n**e. The statue of St. Michael is described as doing human actions: shaking his lance, clapping his wings, etc., as examples of **personification**.

4.   a) Germany is the country referred to in this passage.
        b) Protestantism "tangled" orthodox beliefs by twisting the Biblical texts and inventing new dogmas of predestination and salvation by faith alone (*sola fide*).
        c) There is an **alliteration** with the letter **t**: **t**angled **t**hings, **t**exts.

5.   **And Christian killeth Christian in a narrow dusty room.**
      And Christian dreadeth Christ that hath a newer face of doom.
      And Christian hateth Mary that kissed God in Galilee.
The first line refers to Catholics and Protestants killing each other. The second refers to Calvinists who believed in predestination and a God who could condemn souls to hell for no apparent reason. The third alludes to Protestants who object to Mary's high place of veneration in the Catholic Church.

6. **Spondee/ dactyl/ iamb/ spondee.**

     ′ ‿ ‿ ′ ‿ ‿
7. **Trumpet that / sayeth ha!**

     ′ ‿ ‿ ′ ‿ ‿
    Domino / gloria!

     ′ ‿ ‿ ′ ‿ ‿
    Don John of / Austria

     ‿ ′ ‿ ′ ‿ ′
    Is shout / ing to / his ships.

        a) He is on deck shouting orders to his men, preparing his fleet for the coming confrontation.

        b) **"Domino gloria!"** is translated as *Glory to the Lord!*

STANZA VI (p. 19)
1. Spain and King Philip II. He is the legitimate son of Emperor Charles V and Don John's half-brother. It is clear that Chesterton has a great distaste for Philip from his description of the sickly, unwholesome monarch and household with black velvet on the walls and little dwarves creeping about.

2.   1) **"And his face is as a fungus of a leprous white and gray."**

        2) **"Like plants in the high houses that are shuttered from the day."**

3.   **"Don John's hunting and his hounds have bayed."**

4.   **Gun upon gun, ha! ha!**
            Gun upon gun hurrah!
            Don John of Austria
            Has loosed the cannonade.

    a) Don John has just ordered the guns to fire on the Turkish ships.
    b) The meter is heavy and pounding with consonant and vowel sounds which are harsh and guttural:
        hard **g** and **h**, and short **u**, creating the effect of the boom and recoil of cannon fire.

5.   **Don John / pounding from the / slaughter-paint / ed poop.**

    Scarlet running / over on the / silvers and / the golds.

    Breaking of the / hatches up and / bursting of / the holds.

    White for bliss and / blind for sun and / stunned for lib / erty.

STANZA VII (p. 20-21)

1. The Pope is in his chapel praying.

2. **"He sees as in a mirror on the monstrous twilight sea."** This is the Pope's vision of the battle of Lepanto occurring at the same time.

3. c) chanting, droning, hypnotic. This passage is like an Oriental mantra, a monotonous humming and droning, creating an increasing sense of hopelessness and suffocation.

4. Suddenly the spell is broken with the shout of the men aboard ship: **"Don John of Austria has burst the battle line!"**
    a) The metrical pattern is **dactyl/dactyl/dactyl/iamb.**
    b) **"Don John pounding from the slaughter-painted sloop."**
    c) The verbal adjectives ending in **-ing** are participles.
    d) Using the same verb form throughout this passage gives uniformity and smoothness. The use of
        participles conveys a sense of ongoing action and a sense that the action is occurring in the present.
    e) There are four feet in each line and four strong beats in every line but the first line.
    f) **Alliterations** and **consonances** are both found in this passage. **Alliterations:** the letter **p** in pounding, **p**ainted, **p**oop, **p**urpling, **p**irate's, **p**irate, scarlet, **r**unning, over, silver, breaking, bursting, throng-ing, labor, under, liberty; **th** in **th**rong-ing, **th**ousands, **th**at; **bl** in **bl**oody, **bl**iss, **bl**ind. **Consonances: l** in slaughter, purpling, a**ll**, like b**l**oody, scarlet. silvers, golds.

6. Answers will vary.

7. Like a crescendo in music this stanza increases in intensity until it reaches the climax in Lines 127-137. Then it decreases rapidly in force and excitement to the end where it just fades away.

8.   **Vivat Hispania!**
       Domino gloria!
       Don John of Austria
       Has set his people free!
           a) Long live Spain!
           b) Don John and the Holy League has just secured a great victory and has incidentally freed 2,000 of his own countrymen who were serving as galley slaves on the Turkish ships.

STANZA VIII (p. 21-22)

1. Cervantes fought in the battle and later wrote *Don Quixote* which satirizes the crusading spirit of his time of which he himself had been a part. As Chesterton ironically explains, Cervantes, "the first satirist of crusading romances was one of the last crusaders."

2. **"a lean and foolish knight forever rides in vain."**

3. The poem begins in the Sultan's exotic courtyard where he is smiling as he contemplates his future glory. The poem ends on board a Spanish galley with the wry smile of Cervantes as he imagines Don John riding away into obscurity. Using the same image to begin and end a poem is an example of *inclusion* and is a way of bringing closure to the story.

4. Answers will vary.

LEPANTO TEST
A. IDENTIFICATION
1. Devils.
2. Mahound.
3. Don John.
4. Pope Pius V.
5. Christian galley slave.
6. Cervantes.
7. St. Michael.
8. King Philip.
9. Selim II.
10. Don John.

B. IDENTIFICATION
1. Assonance.
2. Consonance.
3. Simile.
4. Alliteration.
5. Metaphor.
6. Assonance.
7. Alliteration.
8. Simile.
9. Personification.
10. Personification.

C. SCANNING

1.   Stiff flags / straining in / the night / blasts cold.
    B. spondee/dactyl/iamb/spondee

2.   White for bliss and / blind for sun and / stunned for li / berty.
    A. dactyl/dactyl/dactyl/iamb

3.   The North / is full / of tang / led things / and texts / and ach / ing eyes.
    D. iambic

4.   It is Rich / ard; it is Ray / mond; it is God / frey in the gate!
    C. anapest/anapest/anapest/iamb

5.   For that / which was our troub / le comes again / out of the west.
    E. iamb/anapest/anapest/anapest

D. SHORT ANSWER

1. The Turks taking over the island of Cyprus was the event which precipated the Battle of Lepanto.

2. The three European monarchs described in the poem are Queen Elizabe, King Charles IX and King Philip II.

3. Pope Pius V was the pope at the time of the Battle of Lepanto. He was responsible for bringing together the Holy League.

4. The Holy League was an international alliance of men and ships from Spain, Venice and the Papal States under the leadership of Don John of Austria.

5. Rome was known as the Red Apple because it was a large, important metropolis, full of valuable treasures. If it fell, all of Europe would soon follow.

6. The date of the Battle of Lepanto was Oct. 7, 1571. The battle took place in the Gulf of Lepanto which is now known as the Gulf of Corinth.

7. The miraculous event which occurred was the unexpected shift of wind which instead of impeding the Christian forces began blowing in their favor, freeing the thousands of Christians manning the galleys to fight in the battle.

8. The "Sick Man of Europe" refers to the Ottoman Empire which slowly broke up into independent nations at conflict with each other and other countries.

9. Cervantes wrote *Don Quixote* upon his return from the Battle of Lepanto.

10. *The Ballad of the White Horse* was the second epic poem Chesterton wrote in the same year as the publication of *Lepanto*.

E. LITERARY ANALYSIS

／ ◡ ◡ ／ ◡ ◡
Gun upon / gun, ha! ha!

／ ◡ ◡ ／ ◡ ◡
Gun upon / gun hurrah!

／ ◡ ◡ ／ ◡ ◡
Don John of / Austria

◡ ／ ◡ ／ ◡ ／
Has loosed / the can / nonade.

a) The meter of the first three lines is **dactyl / dactyl**.
b) The meter of the fourth line is **iamb / iamb / iamb**.
c) This four-line passage is called the refrain.
d) There are two strong beats in the first three, and three in the last line.
e) There are four strong beats in the other lines of the poem.
f) See answer for this question on p. 38 of the Answer Key, Stanza VI, Question #4.

F. ESSAYS *(Student essays should include most of these details.)*

1. Don John of Austria, the undisputed hero of the Battle of Lepanto, was the illegitimate son of the Holy Emperor, Charles V. He was the half-brother of Philip II of Spain. Though he was young, he was an able leader. In his early twenties he broke up an important Muslim uprising in Spain. Pope Pius V wanted him to be leader of the Holy League because of his bravery, honor and skill at arms despite his obvious youth. Don John was able to take charge of the Holy League from the beginning, and though it was a widely diverse group, kept the coalition together and led them to a brilliant victory. After securing the victory, Don John humbly returned home to Spain where he slipped away from the public gaze and died a few years after the battle of Lepanto, possibly the victim of poisoning by his own brother Philip. The qualities of his we should strive to imitate are his bravery and leadership, but also his humility and his devotion to his Faith which gave him the confidence to undertake such a venture with such overwhelming odds against him.

2. The answers to Questions #1-4 for "The Aftermath" (found on p. 34) will give you a good indication of the details to look for in your student's essay.

ST. PIUS V *(Answers to the optional discussion questions in the student edition)*
CHAPTER ONE
1. His parents were peasants. They were too poor to send him to school so he minded the sheep.

2. He was made Inquisitor General which gave him authority over all the Inquisitors.

3. He was silent and then reluctantly gave his consent.

CHAPTER TWO
1. He ordered the repair of buildings and aqueducts, renewed fortifications, and provided employment and education for the poor.

2. They were a very high priority of his. He used up the funds in the papal treasury on their behalf and during the plague went out himself to give aid to the sick and dying.

CHAPTER THREE

1. He ordered and supervised a thorough reform of the clergy.

2. St. Thomas Aquinas was declared a Doctor of the Church in the pontificate of Pope St. Pius V.

3. There was a great flowering of saints during this time.

CHAPTER FOUR

1. This allowed him to see things as they really were without being distracted by his own interests or motives. His sole aim was to further the Church's honor and glory and provide for the well-being of the Christian people.

2. Cardinal Commendone was Pope St. Pius V's most trusted and competent diplomatic advisor.

3. In his bull *Regnans in excelsis*, Pope St. Pius V declared Elizabeth guilty of heresy, for which she incurred excommunication and forfeited her right to the throne. He declared her subjects no longer bound by allegiance to her and might not lend her obedience under pain of excommunication.

CHAPTER FIVE

1. In this account, Philip II of Spain committed his country to the cause of the Pope and actually paid for half of the cost of the venture.

2. The Turkish invasion of the island of Cyprus was the event which triggered the Holy League's decision to resist the Islamic invaders.

3. Pope Pius V added the Marian title *Auxilium Christianorum,* Help of Christians, to the Litany of Loreto.

CHAPTER SIX

1. The Council of Trent was effective because it actively sought and collected together the true forces of reform, inspired by the great saints of the time: St. Thomas More, St. Ignatius of Loyola, St. Cajetan, St. Angela Merici and St. John Fisher. Its decrees were clear-cut, and penalties for default were well laid-out.

2. The Council of Trent's aim in revising the *Missale Romanum* was to effect unity and purity of faith, worship, doctrine and morals by establishing uniformity of rite and language.

3. It was not a new invention by a small group of experts in the Church but was rather a reestablishment of the Church's most ancient, approved traditions, eliminating any unnecessary accumulations and innovations.

4. The new Missal was welcomed everywhere. There is no record of any widespread reaction against it.

CHAPTER SEVEN

1. The feet of the crucifix which the pope was accustomed to kissing kept moving aside when he tried to kiss them. Pius was overcome with sorrow, thinking that he had become unworthy to venerate the Cross of the Lord. His servants, however, quickly investigated and found that poison had been applied to the feet of the crucifix.

2. The last words of Pope St. Pius V are reported to have been, "Lord, increase my pain, but may it also please Thee to increase my patience."

CHAPTER EIGHT
1. The remains of Pope St. Pius V were interred in the Basilica of St. Mary Major's in Rome.

2. Pope St. Pius V was canonized by Pope Clement XI in 1712.

Made in the USA
Middletown, DE
11 December 2021